MW01248215

Downward Dreaming

Also by Marilyn E. Johnston

Weight of the Angel
Silk Fist Songs
Against Disappearance

Downward Dreaming

poems

Marilyn E. Johnston

GRAYSON BOOKS
West Hartford, Connecticut
graysonbooks.com

Downward Dreaming
Copyright © 2023 by Marilyn E. Johnston
Published by Grayson Books
West Hartford, Connecticut
ISBN: 979-8-9888186-0-1
Library of Congress Control Number: 2023914108

Cover artwork by Marilyn E. Johnston
Book and cover design by Cindy Stewart
Author photo courtesy of Sheryll Bedingfield

Acknowledgments

Grateful acknowledgement is made to these periodicals where the following poems first appeared, sometimes in earlier versions or under different titles:

Alembic: "Unfragmented Fact" and "Heart to Heart"

Atlanta Review: "Daedalus Tying on the Wings of Icarus"

Colere: "Circulation"

Common Ground Review: "Bracelet Gems," "Communion," and "Love Sentence"

Connecticut River Review: "The House We Were Young In"

Earth's Daughters: "Panda Eyes in the Library"

Listening Eye: "Necessity's Blues"

Naugatuck River Review: "To Our Father's Benders"

New Millennium Writings: "A Long Look Back: Resettling Walls"

Penumbra: "Coming to Grips with Cancer," "Father Zeus Descending," and "Misreading *Ezekiel's Vision* by Raphael"

Sulphur River Review: "My Window"

Thema Literary Journal: "Standing in Moondust"

I am grateful to Rhett Watts, Donna Fleischer, Sheryll Bedingfield, and Bettina Viereck for close readings of many of these poems. Also, I wish to thank Ginny Connors of Grayson Books for her devotion to poetry. Her perceptive eye and critical probing made this a better book. Special thanks to Ray for his loving support.

"…be in the difficulty of what it is to be"

—Wallace Stevens

for Rennie McQuilkin

Contents

Free-Wheeling Off Ships

The Imagined Country

Ancestors, you disappeared into the quest
that swallows its own. It was the necessary
migration of gathered selves
toward a new country imagined

when the old one lurched, out-grown, contentious,
writhing with fresh hunger and endless wars,
with walls erected only to be escaped, for a new
satisfying I, on the coastline receding ahead, strand

on which we've never yet set foot—
where everything's still to be achieved,
the people always thirty-five, hard-working,
upholding unwrapped goods or smiles, frozen

beside the car's valiant chrome, the family
in stiff Easter clothes (still imperfect).
I circle in shadows, oddly amiss,
where there is no aim for the living

in the shortfalls of time. I recoil, the past is
unredeemed, many misses, casts in midair.
In terrifying sea-pastures, without a scheme I go,
searching the new ingress, steering my cargo of souls.

Strange Idea of a Family Traveling Through Flesh

I'm thinking of my father today,
shy progenitor, at dawn, fueled by love and duty,
clearing asphalt to provide a way,
wielding self-honed strengths against
self-made obstacles, to build high,
twin mountains of snow at the end
of the Ellington Street driveway. Twin
mounds glistening of ice and gravel
in order to get to work.
I'm off to one side, watching,
yet unseen, as he re-enters the backdoor
and shuffles back out, thin-fleshed,

infant-weak, covered in red and white
bedsores, one lifetime gone. From that dream,
I wake to other images: his pre-war
saloon-owner dad, serene, hand on hip, hailing
and serving, then, his mother's Finnish-laced
speech, long, flowered dress, black shoes,
thick stockings, skinny forearms. Only I turned
to see her face caught in her hands where she stood
frozen on the curb as our Dodge pulled away
at the end of a last Waukegan vacation.

I see his blade cut in, lift, toss
white clouds rolled above his head, as he could, strong
young father, shouldering a family of five
with desires and guilt, the extra load, in pride
of his first burden-castle. How
could he have piled so much, two pyramids
before our eyes? And I, still tunneling down

to deliver my own part: *for the fact remains,*
I'll tell you how, like the fella said, such and such and
such is Life. You don't need to know
what makes you strong
("What's in the bag?" we'd swarm to his hands—
"Fish-hooks!") you just need to bend
to the work beyond your strength even when
the source of strength is gone.

Pages pile up against these walls,
spill in avalanche, then climb back
to get a hearing
beyond failure's last surrendering pitch.

Coming to Grips with Cancer

for my brother, in memory

"Chagall?" he queries the close air.
"Four letters." The daily puzzle in his hands.
I commandeer tactfulness slowly.
"Oh, you know *Chagall*," I cajole. "Just not,

Marc." His silence fills the room.
"You always gave me
more credit than I deserved"
(this, nodding away).

It was fantasy to think crisis
could strip off the old scales

between a brother and a sister
fitted in against seeing one another.
There is still the immovable

blindness in seeing, deafness in hearing
much as there's always been. Throes
of agonized thin fingers
do not change touchlessness.

"Oh, I didn't want to wake uh-up," he murmurs
after a day-long nap: "You just needed
more beauty sleep..." I answer, our old talk
designed for utterance skirting
communication. Then, later,
I know exactly what not to say
when he calls himself "the King of Pain!"

Oh, I would be any kind of sister to him
that he wanted but we are in our childhood masks,
sometimes with glances right to the face
of love that cannot break apart, or hold.

He turns alone on the couch
"...it won't be long now," he groans,
softly, forgetfully—intimately,
to no one in the room
but me.

Daedalus Tying on the Wings of Icarus

after the painting, Daedalus and Icarus,
by Orazio Riminaldi, 1625

The boy urges *Let's go!* pink smooth cheeks aglow,
face craning up, eyes down, sighing
over his father's slowness. Father's
tousled gray wisps fan across
the boy's lush curls. In wide leg stance,
two bodies at a crossroads, Daedalus
reaching behind and around Icarus'
back to affix to new-muscled flesh,
the white-feathered wings of wax.

Their bodies shine bright
against a maze of umbers.
I think of my own inventor-father
at eighty-eight, down to a skeletal body
no heavier than a kite,
unable to rise from his wing chair.

I see my still-strong brother crouch
on bent knee as he inserts arms
under Dad's bird-bone arms and hoists him
doddering to his feet as though restoring a drunk
for a final time, with Ken quipping
"…C'mon, we don't *hug* anymore!"
(they barely touched in life, drunk or sober—).

This is the first and last embrace
        of father and son
as age with illness catches them forever
in a hovering dance toward escape…

They've fallen still a moment now.
Look how the
strapped wings' pale blue ribbons
flutter pitifully
across the firm young shoulders,
cut the heart.

To Open Greater Spaces in the Matter of My Being

I've been resident immigrant in my home,
raking in sheaves of what I have seen, an exile

on a trajectory:
building high to see the foundations

scatter-fade, then bear the ancient redefining.
I bend again to force seeds from the ground.

Note: cultivate the patience of a farmer
for old loves go lost as new ones are found,

for fear grows reckless and turns quick judgment,
sterner. I'd have all be larger for the scope

of what we see in aging
and not settle for life as a boxed-in grumbler.

If I am punished by obtuseness for speaking the heart's core
even as it changes, what was the courage for?

The Conservatory of Emily Dickinson

Fragile pilot-house
a single body wide, lined
with shelves of potted geraniums,
hyacinths, hooks for hanging orchids
on the south-side of the Homestead,
drinking light. Tropical

fragrances could waft
through the door left open
to the dining room. A place
for growing things
all year long—

Didn't have to be large,
a leaf finding the sun in
light-warmed soil, a daffodil
standing in energy's element
all year long.

She must have felt kin
to that glassed-in floating
structure, slightly apart, yet
fixed to, the main house
the plants in rows
all year long.

The inner world facing
nature's outer world
a grid of glass between, beside the brick
rooms on Main Street,
the center to a universe.

Cicadas, butterflies must have
flickered down the glass walls
looking in
their shadows falling over a cascade
of petals: a growing space
of nurturance
large enough for holding in place
a sometimes-shattered heart.

Sister, My Sister

You. Inheritor of all our mother's anxious
gifts in spangle
bags, easing everyone's way, days compiling
five dozen finger sandwiches
for Cousins' Boxing Day.
The tray, a perfect pyramid of thumb-
sized bread squares uniformly aligned
on mandala platter centered with pickles.
Then the curve is thrown: you blurt news
of unearthed cancer cells, scheduled breast
surgery, months of chemotherapy, radiation,
interrupting plans for Myrtle Beach with erupting
medical forms. "All this crap" (your words)
as if we can't be bothered, at this time,
with the first tidal rip of existential
terror. You are focused
moment to moment
and I can't break the mold of so old
a silent language between us.

I moon around, moan. But you press:
"It's simply the most treatable cancer
there is, like Governor Rell's! Stay—
positive!" And I take my worried
eyes down. This is a woman: smile
and bear. Do some *thing*, act, plait,
create, make favors, placemats, anything: bear.
I want to speak of the past.
She has forbidden me to speak.
Now, I have to lead, I rebel.
I say, "...the dinner rolls, the
chocolate chip cookies, bottles of Pinot

and quite a cold spell coming, isn't it?"
Later, it bursts from me: "I'm going through this
with you! I shout, thinking,
but not saying: my way, or, your way,
with you. May we never yield.

Downward Dreaming #1: Mental Dive

Once down, I take off my fins, grip them close
yet walk under the high leafy elms
of the Great Coral Reef. In graceful strides
on the bottom, under bone-branchings
in a watersphere
clear as day. I have the oddest form
among the fitted shapes, gliding
in their own atmosphere.
I walk, though I knew
a blissful flying, for a time.

Schools of shiners pass, out-pace me,
flee and dart. I stand and watch.
I just get by, with the breathing gear
strapped on, the rest of me is human.
Better to go erect in this viscous
element, each step, inch by inch.
Who can say we move
in the coral city any better
than we moved alive in our own space?

I stroll here where immersed
predators out-swim us
threatening. I can only back up,
turn aside, do a few of my learned
maneuvers. For here
I hold my humanity upright,
head on shoulders, heart
on the standby, go
with movement flow swept upon the earth,
daring a dance, even, heel-toe, heel-toe.
The danger of predator fish with big teeth,

daunting. When did my wished-for way lead
into this undersea?
Why did I take off my fins?

Free-Wheeling

The family's perplexed, needling me again:
When ya gonna get on Facebook?
but I have fallen behind my face

holding out for selves not selfies,
reaching for understandings not
smiles before exotic backdrops.

Still, I run my marks the slow way, adhere
to the path of a blue line:
little caterpillars climbing a blue pole. When they reach
the end, they shift left, and start scribbling again.

I don't want life posed, thumbed over,
in lieu. The constant stream
of broadcast life news, distantly
connecting, in lieu.

And if the heart stays unreached,
empty, unappeased?
It's always the first day on your own.
It's always the first day of school.

Standing in Moondust

*"Armstrong's a private person. He is disappointed how quickly
the message of Apollo faded from the minds of men."*
—Hartford Courant, *1988*

What's really important will never fade:

rows on rows of towering sunflowers
bordering the heavily traveled side of Route 5
making an unconsidered mythic frontier
by themselves and the cows
that stand or sit, that languish time
broadside, movements quick only in the ears
and tails and sensitive eyes, blinking—
and words, elegant and rare as ever, fatally
mixed among the plain and readily available
in my brain, and these spontaneous kids
a skinny blond boy this time, white towel
slung from the back of his high bike-seat, looping
circles opposite a friend, on an empty lot
the color of moondust, and a single,
improbable
petunia centering the abandoned
circumference of their tracks
ten yards out at least
from the nearest bed, thriving
in its own dusty sea of tranquility,
starchily unfurled like a breezeless pink flag
still marking, with startling briefness
the sheer longevity of the lonely
message: *I was here.*

Deepening Distance

Corn Men Falling

after viewing Ken Burn's Vietnam

It seemed a suffering Shangri-la and the US
its designated savior, parachuting in
"corn men dropping" like seeds to peasant's eyes.
It reached our home in East Hartford:
Brother drafted to Da Nang, and I, serving
lunches in the town defense plant.

Ken and I argued about life, in high school,
when he scoffed at my books and midnight toil.
He said, "You know, you don't *have to do*
anything!" but then came the draft
and I had to witness his red eyes and soldier's
bearing in the dawn parting for Viet Nam.

We were in over our heads. He returned
jaw-wired, nerves stripped, hot-tempered,
to years of slow growth, evasions
and silence. I came home, too,
to marriage and a life of ideals. But
the corn men kept falling...

Stress of the towers falling
reached Ken on his mail route
with fearful rumors of delivering
anthrax. Cancer was marshalling its forces
inside, warring with the Crohn's.
In vulnerable middle age, in time of war
in a new era of pain, he died
fearing chaos for his teenaged sons.

Hadn't we thought we were beyond that war,
taking up new quests, but no, it went on
burning on a worldwide stage.
We had entered roles and played
our parts, decade after decade,
only to turn as in a long nightmare's sleep
unable to awaken.

Unfragmented Fact

"Being an unfragmented fact—actually your own category"
—Krishnamurti

Land-grant college dorm,
my belongings spread across the floor
all incubated courage mustered
for this new room.
Saying goodbye to parents,
arm around Dad in the photos,
Mom taking the photos, busy organizer,
unpictured in the farewell moment
as it was only Dad's gift to be present
and to master sadness.

On the edge of baggage heaps,
my own space, window frame,
book-case, desk.

By nightfall, I was put off
by the hallway clamor of orientation teams
falsifying everything with cupcakes,
patronizing party games in the lounge.
Balloons? Bags of rhymed nicknames?
I retreated, inwardly cold to it all.

What were clinging girlhood things doing
here, crepe paper hats, stuffed animals, pajama
games to us, the sober ones impatient
for expansion, for the
hard-won entrance into knowledge?

We were straining after possibilities
and the welcome of new selves.

Experiment

I was going to know,
taste what he tasted, Schaefer beer,
one heavy quart of Father's
weekend escape mechanism.

I was going to feel what he felt,
seeking, sequestered, imbibing self away,
bottle after bottle. (What college was for, wasn't it,
trials, stretching identity into growth?)

The thing was dark liquid
amber in space where roommates
played it cool with sliced lemons, ice,
thin packets of strawberry daiquiri.
The room began its spin and I drew in
not transcending, going down,
scientist and explorer, together. It was easy
to watch golden suds disappear

but I could not soar. Never escaped
the Witness hovering over weakness.
Laughter in the beginning, arriving.
merely morose, pinned, flattened on a bed
I sank to the summoning place,

one more happy oblivion
sought after, reached for: denied.
Could he have sought this escape from pain
only to drift toward sleep? I felt the walls
land when my foot crashed the floor.

Autumn

Picking up the sealed envelope of my poems,
my dying brother opens a drawer and slides it in.

Apples lodge on their sides in the grass like meteors.
Lit jack-o'-lanterns in the rain under an umbrella mark my drive.

Drapes of red leaves shake loose
around the gray, denuded maples.

Agent Orange. Did it pursue him down
a fifth decade? He didn't want to know.

To sit alone on the couch, people filing in,
as if passing a child deserted on a playground—

Constant drubbing of a road crew's hammers
like omnipresent grief.

I was gratified, for him, by the gun tribute, graveside,
the unseen bugler of "Taps." Now, I'm not so sure.

The last, best red zinnias flower up
in brown tatters, upright as orphans.

Leaves scatter around him on the wall,
but he sits unmoved, the stone Buddha.

Bracelet Gems

for my brother, in memory

The too-green "emerald" bracelet
packed in the jewel case from high school
stayed as flawless as a remembered Christmas.
I wore it hardly at all in forty years.
Strange that avoidance
of exposing it to wear.
I put it on when he is
dying. It's so lovely, I hold it up
this gift, rare and new, re-presented
unflawed from teenage-hood. Still
shimmering, after all these years.
"Real quality," he nods, approving
his teenage aspiration: *"I'd only buy the best."*
Four years since his death
I've never taken it off.
It is dulling with use,
gold rubbed away, stones glint chipped
by the aching passage of the night and
slow returning of day. How it grips,
all we saved being in life
until later.
Hold me strong
for the world to see
fine, delicate old chain.

Congressional Report

"Ash Carter urged Senators Wednesday to approve an Authorization [to Use Military Force]...against ISIL, interrupted several times by protesters from the anti-war group, Code Pink." —Politico.com, 03-11-2015

Secretary of Defense Ash
Carter and his assistants
lower eyes before the shouting
heckler in Code Pink T-shirt
waving her fragile sign in the middle
of the Congressional floor seating

scrawled characters speaking
in a broken-up play
while the firm muscles of Ash's
frozen frown twitch, his eyes
stay on the page. I know
nothing will change.

Faces of on-lookers register
shades of shockwaves
bewildered dismay
stricken for the Secretary's
lost place, threatened control, everything
unsure—

except the large hands of the bailiff
which gently steer the Protester out
of the picture. Just doing his job.

A freshly-dealt century which began
out of the gate drenched in blood,

for a sixteenth year,
staggers on, blind.

What can we do? Some have gated
communities to fly to, with manmade pools
and lilies floating, when Armageddon descends.
What will protect us from our hearts'
unsafe harbors?

In a New Period of Politics Shorn of Ethics

Alert the children: their daily disinheritance.
Send them a post-card from moral upheaval.

It will take ever-increased artist-strength
to get the message to the center.

I am floating through a doomed department store
where the future will be situated

somewhere in the Aleutians, droning
e-orders onto our backdoor porches in the lower 48.

Life as decorum and comity will be dream
we shared when we failed the sun.

Man, this is not the modern.
Not even the wished-for post-post everything-post-

modern. Think of all the wasted inner space
to be displaced by helmets of virtual reality.

Legacies can't match narrowing ear-buds.
Didn't we inherit and promise to pass on

light? That vow has been subverted.
This is my cry in a dark age.

A Cry to a Brother

for Ken, in memory

Brave imago, you are not here. You
who harangued me receptive and
unreceptive. My face cranes back to your blank cry.

No more Hog River ventures into the wild.
No more go-carts, trout lures, melons stolen from a field.
I'm stripped of your illusions and mine, ready to see the trick
done: How to live without myth and with
a black hole in the center of the universe, like a cancer.
No jousts, no ice-glazed snow forts left.
Maybe both our hearts got crushed in Da Nang
all those years ago and we, no wiser.

My throat stings to hear your: *Storm's comin'. I don't
know where you a-are...*last words of a taped voice mail
I save as the quest falls to one side when the hero dies.

Helpless to penetrate your instinctive gallantry,
watching you hide behind your role as protector.

Life reverts to its worn-heel routine.
My visor lifts, no wearied contender beside me,
as if I had argued a shadow down,
the one sought,
revered, postponed, always, postponed
to the day we'd be together
and there would be
time.

Circulation

I still track my brother
through the lonely adolescent faces
in the library. In black leather jacket,
this one, silent, somber, needs to scan
his diploma and transcripts
for potential dream
employer. I congratulate him
on his graduation
as I would my brother who died
and so things circulate in
this way. He's anxious and fidgety.
A jumble of keys jangles
from a cord around his neck.
Documents mailed, he's
thankful for the attention
for which he appears
astounded and shy.
Wants to know
(holding up coins)
do we have a tip jar?

"Oh, no," I laugh. "No tip jar. Public
Library. You're a taxpayer already…"
The bond flies up on wings
of reciprocated kindness.
We were both startled to deserve it.

Downward Dreaming #2: Quest

"It is only the quest of the mind which cannot be found."
—*Charles Luk,* Ch'an and Zen Teaching, First Series

She began
in Oakwood Acres Project bestowing crushed clover petals
on tin doll plates to invisible congregants gathered of
God, who whispered over her shoulder the liturgy
of the sky-blue healing.

The wind mussed
thin blond hair, a dog barked, the clover
sweet on her tongue. When she stood
a collie careened from the edge, scattering
the dishes, knocking her down amid her offerings.

At ten she acquired schoolmate acolytes
who dispensed ashes rubbed on her bare arms,
as if that was who she was, a shaman's role
behind the family tract ranch in Hartford.

Riddle of God as three-parts
hid in questions, loneliness and smallness
but she was to find her lineage in that story.
She accepted high school and college invisibility
in which she never knew when

she'd be seen. The beginning
merely began. She became
Communications Specialist in the firm,
writing arcane abstracts of the unreal

                    from cubicle to cubicle, behind walls
that never opened out, that grew to higher walls,
                              Alice
down the rabbit hole
                              incommunicado—
She would never break the silence
established in a field of clover.
Now she digs deeper down
in the start of dreaming
as close to childhood
as to wisdom.

Initiation, Again

Swallowing a Pin, a Reprise

At age three, I picked up and swallowed
a straight pin slowly the way someone fixing another's eye

might deliberately drink a cup
of strychnine down, to see what would happen.

I was not aware I was forcing an issue:
something better than nothing?

In one suspended moment
I saw the effect that chance was making

(or chance was living through)
in the center of the room, Mother

dropping a vacuum hose,
her shocked face

floating right up to my eyes
a searching look of helpless terror

when I was already gone.
The hospital: light-stripes of black crib,

body emptying one night-long wail into dark:
my space in the family closed.

How strange feeling this memory again, unbidden—
so many years later.

What was in my mind that took up that pin, and staring
traced my lips like a prayer, like a consecration?

Idle Design

One tub of water, Sunday nights—
I was third, adding more hot
from the tap's thundering pour.

I lay back, watching pink walls soar
to the ceiling, drew up one knee,
soaped a wet washcloth,
to a lump of saturated clay
plopped it on that knee,

then scooped, pulled, arranged,
styled the "hairdo" on this opposite head
as I pleased, for as long as I wanted,

traced under it a mouth and two eyes
in the suds on the smooth skin—
Even in this, making, creating,

even in this, engaged,
imagining, bringing the visible
from the invisible. Didn't matter if it was

idle play, fleet as soap.
I made a head and face
out of anther week's passing nothingness

with an intimation of Something, beyond.
I suppose those eyes opened
happily at the sight of me

whole, by design.

Vacuum Core

What nature abhors, we sometimes choose
to inhabit. To pull out and hug loss
to ourselves like a stuffed rabbit from age nine
to too long in the dark. Filling a space
entirely devoid of matter,
vacuum empty, a process place,
an apparatus for drawing up, erasing.
to get behind a vacuum cleaner,
a safe place. The focus
restricted to a single path at the feet,
other things out of sight.
The vacuum sucked the child away.

The girl became used to flashing signals
that were not picked up.
She became
a non-speaking part.

The family, a conundrum
tightly-knit that clung together, silently.
The child saw the blank in their midst
was herself and began to fill the space
with lines of words
she inscribed with a roaring pen
her only is: words, glinting backwards
on the forward-moving line.

Heart to Heart

This day could write itself before-
hand. The heart will enter clutching
its one riotous bouquet of zinnias
in hot colors. Mother's shyness

will step forward awkwardly:
to be kissed. Eyes on the flowers.
They will need a vase then. There
will be the dance around the vase.

There will be the manifest turn
to many common objects in the room.
Then, the garden will have more hard reality
than the heart will feel for itself.

Talk will begin and last all day
and it will, again, stave off
all there is to say. They will
eat lunch, they will share tea

and comment on everything visible.
This is to avoid entering depth-
holes of lost ones who opened vacancies
in the beginning of a new century.

At fifty-nine, the heart feels hollow
as though stepping onto an empty stage.
Like memory in a February garden
things become entirely potential:

Mother's roses by the split-rail
full, brave, brimming
clear in 1961. Heart to heart
we haunt each other.

Communion

Mother, widowed four years, walks my orchard path
notices two slim leaves protruding from the ground.

"Lily of the valley?" We cross the threshold of Ray's barn:
"Should I wipe my feet?" she jokes.

We study the clean workbench, the radio
left playing to entertain the mice, the yellow canoe

riding aloft his '64 Ford which was rolled in
twenty years ago and (let's face it) is never to be driven out.

Then we wander to the pond's edge
to study the rotted willows and the daylight silence of the hylas

and then she steps into my field of nothingness—
with me. How soft our walk over mown

straw reeds faint of her childhood farm, to the very center
a single cedar tree and a stand of pussy willows.

We can't reach above the dead branches
for the new fur buds halfway to frizz.

We are in the field of nothingness
and there's nothing we need to get.

Two women
who enjoy walking untilled earth.

My nature has unfolded here, I would explain,
if I could, *that's what the field is for.*

And she would stoop to probe an up-thrust stick of green
and go through the trials of finding its name.

We are in the field of nothingness, Mother,
and there's nothing we need fix.

Be with me. Nothing left
to strain for, nothing from missed time or its marks.

Downward Dreaming #3: The Sofa

"I slapped your hand
in my dream last night—" Mother's shy report.
"I said, get away from that laundry:
I will do it myself!"

Then, she told me of the dream
about her sofa in the living room,
which three years ago, at 91
she tried to lift in order to clean behind
(her "accident" she still calls it)
which led to surgery at 92, added ten years
to her old age, and set her on
this stupid cane. "I dreamed
I was standing by that sofa, shoving it off
and I was telling someone, *oh, it hasn't been*
moved in years, and then
I picked it up so easily," she said

and we bent in to trace the drifts
behind, peering into "dust, pencils,
mounted-up paper, trash, dirt,
all kinds of hidden debris…"

Mother and Her Youngest Child

"Oh—this—hair!" she scorns the mirror I hold up.
"Oh, Marilyn!" she whispers, overwhelmed with keeping alive.

"I'M YOUR MOTHER!" orders me off her treasured tasks.
"I don't think you should come here anymore." Later:

"I'm sorry. Sorry. Forgive. And forget?" she wails,
"I'm used to being independent," glossing defiance.

Snaps the old cake carrier lid on her imperfect cake.
She can do her OWN laundry, begins again those treacherous stairs.

"I can't stay alone!" her widowed wail, fifteen years.
"It is what it is—" she surrenders.

"I can't tilt my head for these damn drops!
It's one thing after another, going wrong."

"I won't wear that alert button, NO!" her face is set.
"It reminds me I'm alone. I KNOW I'M ALONE!"

Why must we fight about everything! my outburst, lost.
Mother-daughter off known ground, agonized.

Igniting each other's angers as in childhood shames, the fuel;
the future unclear, loose mystery, mother and her youngest child.

I used to want her to see me!
Now time laughs, strips us to shredded masks,

unable to budge, hands tied, tongue-tied. I tell myself:
Heart, you break differently from her, away from lies.

Just tell me what you want! "There comes a time when you can't do anymore:" her first admission.

"I've got a job for you," she announces at last. And I do whatever she asks, loving, floundering, pitying. Daughter.

Girl Scientist

Still she floats, explores, tries, comes to nothing
not even decades of writing pinning thoughts down.

There was that prize won at the Armory Fair
for mixed solutions, test tube colors pegged in a spectrum.

Investigating no different in deep space
where she imagines herself now, nights

without days. Days of floating,
in and out, subject to the nearness of the earth.

But it's been brought to her attention, feet on floor:
gravity is not a force of the earth pulling us in,

but rather a long slide over bulge-creased spacetime,
everything careening by slants to a downward dreaming,

moving in free-fall which by sudden acceleration
connects feet to the floor and we begin again. Simply a trick

to walk the dirt-packed earth. There are tasks
to be done in this alteration of motion and stillness.

Phenomena to analyze: cycles
rolling to a stop first sent moving eons ago.

Every face turned her way is different now
and doesn't know her ever-shifting face.

She is not rising or setting. And she does not have to
keep her laboratory leaping through narrative arcs.

There was that card table she set up
in shadowy lights by the basement stairs,

the work that followed with batteries, light bulbs and magnets,
the force clothed in iron filings. She keeps trusting to that.

Free, on the cusp of discovery partially resolved
in these bonds she so desperately clings to, but cannot secure.

Memory Engrams

Evidently, we're reducible to these:
engrams, millions of neurons
holding memory in the brain, traces
that flood in, like swinging in maple boughs
or offering crushed clover petals
on tin plates to the sky, or tracking
birds across the cloudscape vistas.
I have never left that field,
the clouds at my feet, that space
where intuitive acts of praise took place:
shaping cakes out of mud,
tracing fireflies in the dark of 1955.
We turn and yearn after that first sound
of the chickadee's *who-who?* A call

to stare up into the down-searching
sunflower's gaze, a flower's
sympathy, breathing one in,
mustiness under the front-stoop,
cutting teeth into the acrid orange-half
round as the sun toying with yarn loops
meaningful, then, like
loops of scented petals falling in loose
braid. This was the first field behind
Oakwood Acres'—paths winding
to shady woods to the convent
of the sisters and their pastured cows.

I have never left that field
but carry it with me, even to the coldest
vacuum—as memory stays memory
of home, the run I take into the field

turning to take one whole look back, arms flung
to embrace to the fullest expanse holding
oppositions trembling within one cherished life.

Initiation, Again

Under three and a half decades of clutter
at one address, the hundred-year-old house
stands below the running rim of Talcott Ridge.
Atop that prehistoric ridge, Metacomet Trail,
where King Philip ran out to the end of his
answers. He ended tortured,
head on a fencepost at a Simsbury fort.
His people became a ridge trail name
running from here to the Chesapeake.
This house planted deep
in ridge shadow
where I've set an easel in the
tall-windowed basement
and pens and notebooks in the upstairs
room. Waiting to be tapped.
Chaos grows toward the center of each space.
I've saved memory in a folded ocean
of neurons. And I've forgotten
the purposes that drove passion.
                                    The trees
grow past the windows. The ridge
still runs away. I step outside in space.
I am one with all this, again
the self who withers under her rings
toward renewal.

Odd Duck Blues

Weeping Cherry

"For she was the maker of the song she sang…"
—Wallace Stevens

Young woman long-misplaced
exhausted by climbing up
ladder rungs, misaligned

in her three-hundred-dollar suit
limping with fatigue and fate,
carrying the cards, the flowers and the boxed cutlery,

corporate gifts for fifteen years
of sacrificed dream life, sliding through doors
onto the corporate bench, false

smiles bidding goodnight.
Where was she going? Bare tiles
rocked her by the open hallway.

Her back to the wall, she studied a life
plastered over with paychecks.
It was the end of a journey, or something
of a beginning of a re-beginning.

Then, she saw it: exploding pink
in its glass-bound courtyard,
the soft soaring crown cresting the stories,
still standing where it had grown up in gravel
under its square of sky, the motionless clouds—
boxed-in by reflections.

The tree waved from its place.
She heard it: *there never was a world for her*

except the one she...made. She rose on this. It was time to leave.

Downward Dreaming #4: Fantasy Life

Enough of racked cubicles,
oblong manuals, oblong papers, oblong screens
by the square-shouldered coffee machine.
You quit all that to jump-cut summer,
to study the background ladders: mother/daughter,
daughter/father, brother/sister,
sister/sister. You burrowed to the source:
the thing you wanted to be to them
that they couldn't see
and the thing you appeared to be to them
that you couldn't accept as yourself.

You couldn't escape, unless it was to step out
somersaulting into the void—
making good on a riddle overtaking a worn-out
pledge, to be yourself.

And then, you moved motionlessly
clanging through the turn-style
of male desires day by day,
layer by layer, exploring looks
like something was going on
while something else was fading.
The returning looks
and the on and off movement in stasis
of emotional affairs became the substance
from which self-knowledge was made.

Something climbed up to show itself
standing here, self-asserting, making land
speak itself in the sea of self-restraint.

Instrumental

for my father, in memory

Where did it come from, that violin
lifted tenderly from its velvet case
on the rec room floor and held high
in rare performance that came and vanished.

He nestled chin on the chin rest,
his tall bulk on the couch edge,
knees spread, torso leaning forward,
face a study in serious

concentration like a star in a philharmonic.
Those workman's ham-hock fingers
danced on four delicate strings
or swiftly plied the bow which he'd rosined

lightly with an amber stone...
I know he'd never had a lesson
but what he taught himself
a lilting jig, one foot tapping,

or improvised a sweet melody vibrant
with sorrow.
He conjured and listened close,
inviting it forth, that violin,
to speak *violin*. He played by ear.
He did that with everyone.

A Long Look-Back: Resettling Walls

She yearned for a nameless chaos
under her calmly-ordered life, needed
some turmoil close to home
to see what torment might be like, to ache

after a new face, for example, but safely,
from a closed center
while desires danced along the outer ridge
she could run towards and back from,

safely. She needed life, at root, at peace
on the backs of the furies, two lives
at once. To feel risk
of desire against the home threat

of eternal sameness wrenching
a core in two, in a comfortable room,
scanning room rent ads on a Sunday morning
because her home had lifted off

its sills and soared and remained floating
and she could fear the true-partnered life forever
too thin, and life wrenched unmoored as a weed
sliding sideways atop breaking waves...

as real as anything she'd ever feel
and yet, staying in the only life she could live.
Inevitably, when reality
settled back down

and she seemed to know what from
what, she received life

back, whole: walls, floors, ceilings, roof
fitted, her own, with one incongruous past

storm receding, roiling on to other homes
of husbands and wives entering their forties.
Now she takes up time enriched by
poise, at home again, moving with the shimmers.

To Our Retirement

for Ray

Retirement, I'm humbled by your mystery...
word games and multiplying chores
have got us, have got Ray. His other steady
companions now: a Webster's, a Colliers,
four language dictionaries (including music) and the world
of googling one word-prize at a time...

You hold him fast, routine puller
into the arms of the *Hartford Courant*
every weekday morning
habitual, without fail. He sits with coffee,
pencil, eraser and the old pre-work ritual
that lasts, on escape breaks, all day, until the next day
when the answers arrive at dawn
with a fresh batch of crossword blanks ready
with clues. You have entered our lives
at a touch, transformed us anew—
I bow to the power you wield, Retirement:

you have stripped and focused a context
to basics, to love and the maintenance of love
and its house, the cushions of a home library
and his dead mother's sun-porch chaise,
a career pared away but what's left absorbs him
in grids of trivia and Modern Marvels, natural,
historical, electrical, mechanical, and internal-
cumbustional. He stokes industry with unlimited time
to fix up, shore up, sand, paint, plant the homestead
for a woman's praise. Time is absence and what
can now be on stage, with hidden purpose
but maintenance of another's happiness.

"Retirement is complicated!" I worried aloud one day.
"It is?" he looked up, stumped. *"Oh yes,*
it is." I beg for what you are withholding
oh terrible, curious, insatiable Retirement,
in your riddle.

Next Planet

Learn to cultivate a sturdier Zen.
Wear no pressable buttons.
Lose yourself
in music while playing music.
Ask for a brain that doesn't over-think
thinking. Practice one art
and take all the time it needs.
Be an expert at something.
Be the one others rely on.
Try to be first-born, next planet,
strong, fearless, calm,
the cooler head prevailing
in the crises. Stop being the one
third-questioning, second-guessing.
Next planet, it would be good to be
unashamed of sensuality.
Dance whatever you want to dance.
Follow bliss to the very end
and reincarnate in good judgment.
Travel to faraway places
not as a tourist but as fearless observer
on a pathless path
to the moon
or to an unmapped Mars,
happy and confident,
finding your own way.

Colchester Point, Vermont

There hang the green cherries on three stems
conjoined at the top to one twig
fitted to one branch, fitted to a trunk.

Oak leaves flow on currents of wind
shiver in a revelation of light
bracing, high, upheld and free.

Climbing the hill, the berm falls away
and there it is: the white
frond of white petals trembling
above a black stream,
there all along, seen or unseen.
Currents of wind, flower heads
weighed to earth by blossoming.

The dripping rain polishes dark
willow leaves darker carved
in their place in the light
twirled over a churning lake.

Necessity's Blues

"...nature is never spent;
There lives the dearest
freshness deep down things..."
—Gerard Manly Hopkins, "God's Grandeur"

Nothing better than a sad tune
We make our music rue
We understand a sad song
We make our music rue
If we were singing Eden's dawn-break
we'd be singin' that song blue...

We didn't make life easy
We called it sweat and toil
We didn't make life easy
We found but sweat and toil
I've seen the vision dry up
before the goods were spoiled

I've seen through daylight empty
knew not why or how
I've seen through daylight empty
knew not the why or how
Worked for God to hear me
Don't know why I'm workin' now

A freshness, deep down things?
I'd be the last to know
If there's a freshness deep down things—
I'd be the last to know
Get so turned around behind time
There's no place for me to go

We like our silence, don't we?
Well, there's something ain't been sung
We like our silence, don't we?
There's something ain't been sung
You keep on singin' baby
Out where the heart is flung

Hanging in Mid-Air

Clouds pile up
before the high-piled
hills, blue-gray bordering
the steel-waved lake.

Cutting straight through the sky,
dark weeping willow fronds
trail on the wind
like sky hooks, like sky verdure

dangling, the trunk
assumed, but all in all
one system, one heart
of life tossed by the wind.

This is growth lost to itself
save for the reaches of
hope and the green
tree-remembering sky.

Standing on Becoming

Deep Eye on Surface

She used to be small
able to hide
in protective flesh.
Flesh has grown thin,
the living exposed.

She used to hide
in fantasies interwoven
with the fantasies of
others: all those characters
gone, though cried for. Time

wears through all hiding
and she is left
vulnerable alone. Standing
in space, being what's left of being
seen. How do we go on—

resisting, yet
loving the eroding wind?

To Our Father's Benders

You were reliably unreliable
in your surprise, shattering
the steady work week, offering the open door,
free of time, identity uprooted, then, returned...

Mom kept you in check with Saturday
night drinking, neighbors and cards
or just herself and basement TV dancing bubbles.
But every six months or so

explosion of what had been
excluded would have its sway,
wrenching prolonged attention
on you! You led the wayward way

from home, like a child evading
politeness and clocks. A rebel
in the locks. Your question,
above every other question,

your due above all other dues!
Unreliably reliable. Surely there was
the clean work shirt, pressed pants waiting
fresh-brewed coffee, soft-talk to an outer ear.

Yet, at precisely the wrong time—
you brought him, staggering, a man of dismay
rattling every shining cup and perfect rose
flouting Mom's tight-lipped horror and dry-eyed calm.

To be creative at all, to dive into depths
against which a self is defined,
then re-crafted, resurfacing…
you needed something beyond the sane

fulfillments, a plunge,
reaching to a sheered-off gaunt
exhaustion, something like that, your due
exacted and paid—in excess,

before he could crawl back
into service devoted to nothing
but the dull life of loving us again
with his full heart unstintingly pouring.

Father Zeus Descending

Hera brushes an arthritic knuckle
against his empurpled hand, fusses, strains,
frightened, as if this were not her husband
but her life, long-fought-for, beloved, dissolving.

The dreamed daughter stands looking on
for his knowing look, eyes lost. The old man coughs
makes no other sound, as if slipping into a mid-life binge
he's let slip too far, this time.

In my golden sandals ties unlaced
upon the floor, I'm Athena
by the nursing home window where leaning iris
cannot right themselves, stripped of blooms.

Oh, when he was still himself, he could lift his chin
and seek our admiration, feed us the food we craved:
"Cut my meat small" he calls from the lamb skin
pad. O father, where has our mountain gone?

Brood over your dark star collapsed before TV,
breath muffled under an oxygen mask.
Each day, how your mythic mind pressed into mine,
out-folding, folding until stillness joined to stillness.

Misreading *Ezekiel's Vision* by Raphael

"Whither the spirit was to go, they went..." —Ezekiel, Verse 4

This was what I first snared in faulty seeing:
a man, seated among winged bearers, not rising
but rather on the backs of wardens
with animal faces and snarling mastiffs
carrying him down, arms up-flung
like a winning coach carried to earth in victory.

Fear led to my mis-seeing,
led me to the mastiff's jaw,
clamping and growling in dissent.

Life now all descent, a senselessness
peeling away at images. An anti-vision
rocks before my eyes, smells
of the chewed over, spat out massacre of children.

The necessity of faith and love hides.
The human now seems only a silverfish
in the lower left-hand corner of the canvas,
the decay of God in a dream.

Down to Their Very Lack

to my father, in memory

Spirit, I send you no farther.
                              I mean, yes, you're in
Sister's and Brother's children and their
children's children

but not in that precise blend of you and me otherwise
                         possible if I had had children of my own.

"Children of my own"—those malleable words
            bend now to new meanings
as a life of choice burns in a last look at a single branching
                    over time.
"Childless" stays a sign, missing a referent, a riddle,
negligible to the mind,
                yet still the children I never had
                    haunt my imagination,
take on weight, add substance to their meaning through time
to be felt, at last, children of my own,
                down to their very lack.

                    Spirit, that I have prized for my whole life:
go on flowing forever to your
                              unknown end—

I do not know
                where our wandering spirit stops
                              when I die.

Downward Dreaming #5: Becoming Nothing

The legacy of many decades is still self-incredulity.
      I must re-find the child
in hooded yellow slicker and great red boots
who burst out of the side of Father's
      rec room bar, shouting and clomping and
strafing the imponderable circle of brother and his friends

with a Dadaist's uproar! A no-thing—
to be seen! A happening first
      to her own belief, elusive in a backstage life.

Now it's life in company, suppressing words,
      in favor of another's monologue,
or sit, alone, with animated
      books and window ornaments
wondering when this voice will come into its speaking.

      Today the Christmas tree, lit, once in forest magic,
looks already dead still tinsel-trimmed
on its inevitable trip to the sidewalk.

                      Being
is to be in an empty theatre, amid the everyday, cast down.
I'll have to kick upwards again to the fertile element.
      I must belong to the child again
      swinging off branch-ends into air.

Silent Screen Actress

When all was silent, silence was a language,
every gesture expressive, magnified, lived.
And I flowed in that medium, a meaning
when every look and head shift was thought.
Then entered: the talkies' big-bang vocalizations.

Only then was thought relegated from
that cut-away stare that meant *thought*, to fleeting
interludes of speeches at one remove.
My life could be captured on silent film:

all smiles or eager eye appeals,
body language, ideals
enfolded in begging hands or craning back
to unspoken wants no one can interpret.

I loved mostly in repression before
life shredded into sound—
knew my heart died in words.
And color? Color killed me cold.

What next? 3-D? Interactive?
Hologram, am I even here?
The actress you were looking for
patterned out in words, is gone.

My Window

A curtain of drops sheathes the window,
before bolts of yellow leaves, athwart the shining
lichen-spotted branches rain soaked black.
Rain taps its remorseless code
from the sky. Earth takes it all in, translates:
What else is possible? Delicate webs of clouds
lose shape to farther clouds, spokes
of sun arabesques. Will you wait in your corner
for the next disappointing word?
It will come. It will stand and stab
more durably than any wished-back love.
Do we need words only to track shadowy longings
or to encode umbrage taken with this world?
There it is, thrill of a wound.
We make a place for it to come in. We want
outrage. It says we are tragic and must mean
something. Still, I think I envy that flock
of starlings that races and flares up with one cry
over yellow field, a thinly-woven scarf without breaking.

Day Off from Grief

Oblique lines of flying birds arrow down to the field.

You have emptied your rucksack
on the narrow grass

white flutterings: lines, crammed between lines beyond
the margins of poems, lines scribbled
        straight across the typeface of other poems:

How many times do I have to tell you...
       Keep your trap shut!
                I'm not going to tell you again (Dad)

Home. You can see anonymous vines
infiltrating the prickly hedge behind

the stone Buddha: grape leaves drape him
in rows of pale shriveled handkerchiefs.

You are fleeing the weight of the subtracted,
a father's back retreating

to disappear before the child's
longing to please, to please, to please

and the unused love comes back as though from a dead person.
It's true: maybe you *don't* have enough selves

to go around salving the needs of the dispossessed,
but comes a time in late afternoon in mid-August

that the past, brimming with unfulfilled futures begins to shred
and you lie down, lawn-still, resolved never to give

another feeling, another single word, not another thought
even the slightest nod, to anybody—

then, you start up, thinking of someone else
and what you might do for them, and you rise and move on.

Panda Eyes in the Library

Dominic enters, wearing his panda hat:
white knit skull topped with black-bear ears,
two black-rimmed eye-holes pulled up on his brow.
I'm going to have call you four eyes, I say.

No, you can't. He yanks
panda eyes over his glasses.
He comes here to escape the world.

We two on a plane of discourse we share instantly
no one else aboard
and always the terrorists trying to kick us off.

Come to the open mic!
Don't you write? And he shows me
a poem...in his scribbled hand about dashing fate.

It's strong. Who writes about fate anymore?
Nobody that's who, I say. "You mean," young and sad,
he launches into his best youth imitation, "it's all:
bee bop to the hip hop to the flash dash
slap blab, fist to the crisp into the ocean of emotion?"

and we laugh. He looks at me
from out of his panda eyes, then
shakes my hand, walks out the backdoor,
descending again to the far-east forest he hides in.

An Infinite Worker

is building boundary-less-ness,
tilts her head and reads
letters from Aristotle, wrestles
with Nietzsche's *herd*
vs. the *Overman*, sits and compares
white-on-white snow
with clouded sky over snow field,
sits and watches the snow clumps
give way from the highest fir branches,
clipping in flight the lower snow-clumps
that fall also into
            ...boundary-less-ness—

It's falling and transferring from life
into books of heroes falling down rabbit holes
off ships like Vaino's sailing to Pohja,
or that of Odysseus sailing to Troy,
from Troy to Dublin, from Dublin
to Oz. I myself am fewer than ten miles
from the ground
of my first disappearance into head-high straw
of Oakwood Acres now vanished under West Hartford
sprawl, all flights by foot then, mind to future, future
to past, heart tethered to a vanquished signpost.

Ego's a mind tool, mind-made adze
amid other tools of intellect, shaped in the small reader,
the younger self, a child of a larger fate dictating

boundary-less-ness,
which we are ever climbing through as we
climbed saplings on the edge of

the woods to be a swinger of
maples first, before riding black branches
up snow-white trunks of paper birches...
                                    I've slid off that ride
onto this one, settling to construct
this worker's life, building up
boundary-less-ness, a state so long tested
through temptations down to the standing
trial of questing, requestioning, then faltering,
then knowing.

Poetry Reading Series Sorcerer

You remember what it takes to cast spells:
fragrant coffee, field flowers, chairs in a half-circle.
It's to be an evening of bouquets and fresh-cut poetry
and the lotus lifts her head above the mud.
There'll be inward speech in full abundance

glances, pledges, sorrowing, sighs.
The whole human show in poems
unfurled past the lighting of the peace candle
so the dead will not be left behind, wondering
where life has gone out for the evening

not thoughtless of them, not forgetting.
I'll try to say: this is for your Ears, yes,
to talk to you, remember? How else, but
inside every word. The spirit in the letter—
You were the first to tell me

of the dog struck down in the street howling
and of the chicken and the egg of gentleness and violence
on your dull Rutherford prescription pads: Speak! *Oya!*
The past is for those who lived in the past...

Yet, here we gather the living and the dead,
listening in the circle I've stood in twenty years—
knowing words must save and there's no future in silence.

Georgia O'Keefe in New Mexico

If you marry a consciousness
alike but different from your own
why should it mean
you don't get to live married
to your own perceptions?

I throw more blank canvases in the back
with the painting tools, drive out
to the Santa Christo mountains.
When the sun gets high

I crawl inside for relief,
use this Model A as respite
studio, out here, in the center
of the desert. The days are mine.

The songs of the coyote
thrilling across the sand, mine, the road
runner's songs, my songs.
I know the solitude of the cactus.

I have come two thousand miles
to the transparent air of New Mexico
to feel this unmarried, married, to escape
the unexamined atmosphere,

to breathe in the simplest way here,
queen of space with my own
implements, the weather, the desert,
these red hills,

adobe brick warmed under the sun's wheel
and that skull riddled against saturated blue,
filled to intensity
with silence and communion.

The House We Were Young In

we bought from Evelyn and Edwin Brown,
who'd lived and raised five children
in the four small rooms for forty years
before us, loved, worked, sickened
departed for the Millstone Retirement
Home. "Brownie," that first owner,
strolled back every week to Spalding Circle
paying tribute to the shining
symbol of his past. "Don't work so hard!"
(don't change it) he seemed to plead with his hands.
But it was our start-up, we changed it:
the white clapboard to slate blue aluminum,
brass lights and mailbox
by the front door and took down
whole walls inside. Even lifted the roof
inserting a full dormer on top,
conjuring a dream from a magazine:
French wallpapers, a four poster,
a writer's table, Franklin
stove. The house we were young in

improved with us. I watched you
skitter down the cement stairs
of the cellar bulkhead, hammer in hand
a thousand times, or seated, limbs akimbo
weeding the plot of tomatoes, rounding
the house corner on your bike,
or shirt off, cutting, planing
the rough-hewn floorboards
in our upper room. I remember
I could clean that thirties' Cape
in an hour then take the rest of the hours off

to type one poem's worth of
a hundred drafts. And every day
ended with the two of us
tucked in bed by the tree tops
by the east-facing window
under the exhilarating, comfortable stars.

Love Sentence

He is. She is. They love, they
live. They work: they build
a house. She builds a sentence.
He maintains the house and she maintains
the sentence, mending it for
softening, leaks, interior damage,
both balanced against the pitch-prone,
serving and righting things in renovation.
He watches the house grow
as she watches the sentence grow
by mounting steps, parallel construction.
That is her job. That is his job
to put the walls up
against chaos, to live in the house,
into meanings of a house underneath
the house and
inside the materials, words,
nails and beams, floor to
ceiling joists, creating space
creating a home in which they
capture the flow of their hearts and find
Time enough for time
to make mute chambers sing.

Generational

At a picnic table, older mothers, with some weight,
settled by life, in a bunched row, hair cropped,
bemoaning work and the next child's wedding costs
and next to them, the young, long-haired, single nieces,
in a loose ring on separate lawn chairs, matured
but reluctant to add to that settled group table. I am host

of this picnic. I take the Adirondack chair
adjoined to one end of the Mother's Bench
but slyly aligned to the circle of youth.
I'm included in neither one, but older, married
and childless, am the bridge, the hinge, the bolt.

These older mothers face the future with their backs,
as if to temper time pouring slowly
over their shoulders and down into their
surprised empty laps. The unattached women

lounge expansively, limbs draped in leisure,
facing unknowns with alert languorous language,
minutely manicured, pampered bodies,
waiting, waiting to build, venture, quest—

Surely something new will come to us!
Surely something strong like fate will come
ripe with the challenges of fulfillments exactly
commensurate to our watchful, generous lack.

Unquitting

January First, again, Robinson Crusoe
on an island. Having to make your own spoon.

Scavenge for food. Water. Shelter.
No paper to write on. Paper more

useful as the inner sole
of shoes. How to get through

January 2. The heroes? Your faith
in them? Their mangled lives implying

yours? The best of what they tried to do
implying your best. They didn't quit

until circumstances overthrew them,
papered over with deeper meanings. The back

of an envelope. Scrap of a scribbled napkin,
seed ideas stuffed in a drawer,

life lines. It's not enough, life alone.
You want the heart meeting the hermit's word.

You have to lose yourself in survival craft
and nature's gifts. You could die any day.

You could learn to be ready. You have it still ahead,
the getting lost. You have to leave a trail.

Notes

"Strange Idea of a Family Traveling Through Flesh:" The title is a phrase from the work of Elizabeth Bishop.

"To Open Greater Space in the Matter of My Being:" The title is a phrase from the work of Primo Levi.

"Weeping Cherry:" The epigraph and the line *There never was a world for her except the one she...made* are taken from the Wallace Stevens' poem "The Idea of Order at Key West."

"An Infinite Worker:" Vaino is the main character in the Finnish epic myth *The Kalevala*. Pohja, from the same epic, is the northern place of challenges and quests.

About the Author

In addition to *Downward Dreaming*, Marilyn E. Johnston is the author of two other books of poetry, *Silk Fist Songs* and *Weight of the Angel*, both published by Antrim House Books. Her chapbook *Against Disappearance* won publication as a finalist in the 2001 poetry competition of Redgreene Press. She holds an MA in English from Trinity College. Her poems have been widely published in such journals as the *South Carolina Review*, *Worcester Review*, *Poet Lore*, *bottle rockets*, and *Rattle*. Her honors include six Pushcart Prize nominations. In 1996, she co-founded the still popular Wintonbury Poetry Series in Bloomfield Library, which she ran for twenty years. She lives in a 100-year-old farmhouse on four acres in Bloomfield, Connecticut with her husband Ray.